The Story of
CAPE COD

by
Kevin Shortsleeve

Illustrated by
Elka Iwanowski

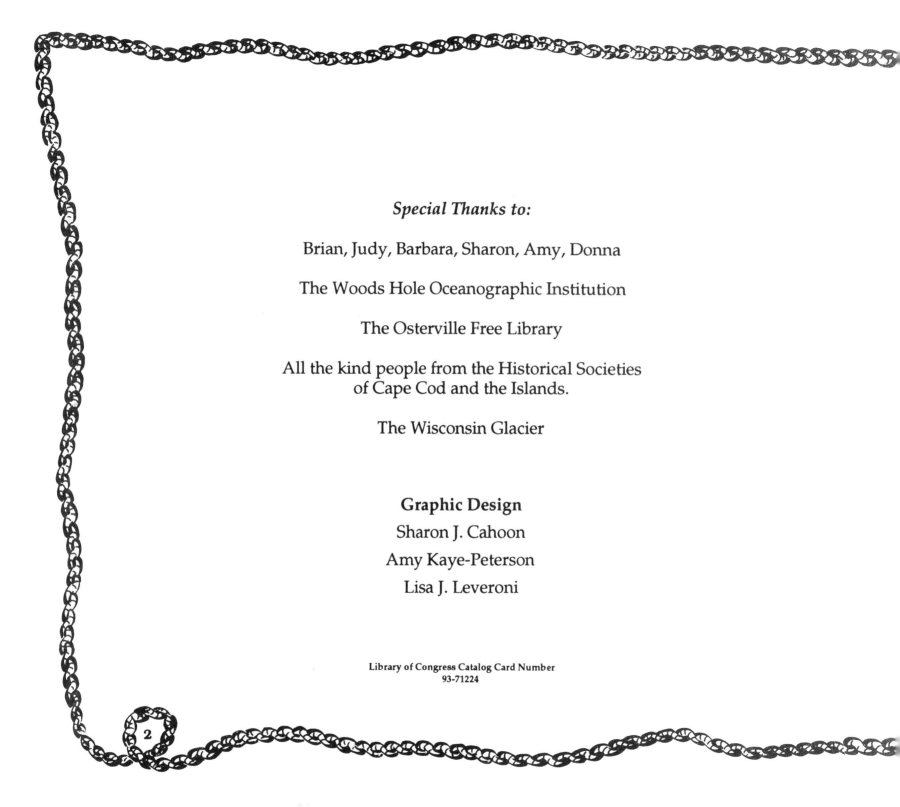

Special Thanks to:

Brian, Judy, Barbara, Sharon, Amy, Donna

The Woods Hole Oceanographic Institution

The Osterville Free Library

All the kind people from the Historical Societies
of Cape Cod and the Islands.

The Wisconsin Glacier

Graphic Design

Sharon J. Cahoon

Amy Kaye-Peterson

Lisa J. Leveroni

Library of Congress Catalog Card Number
93-71224

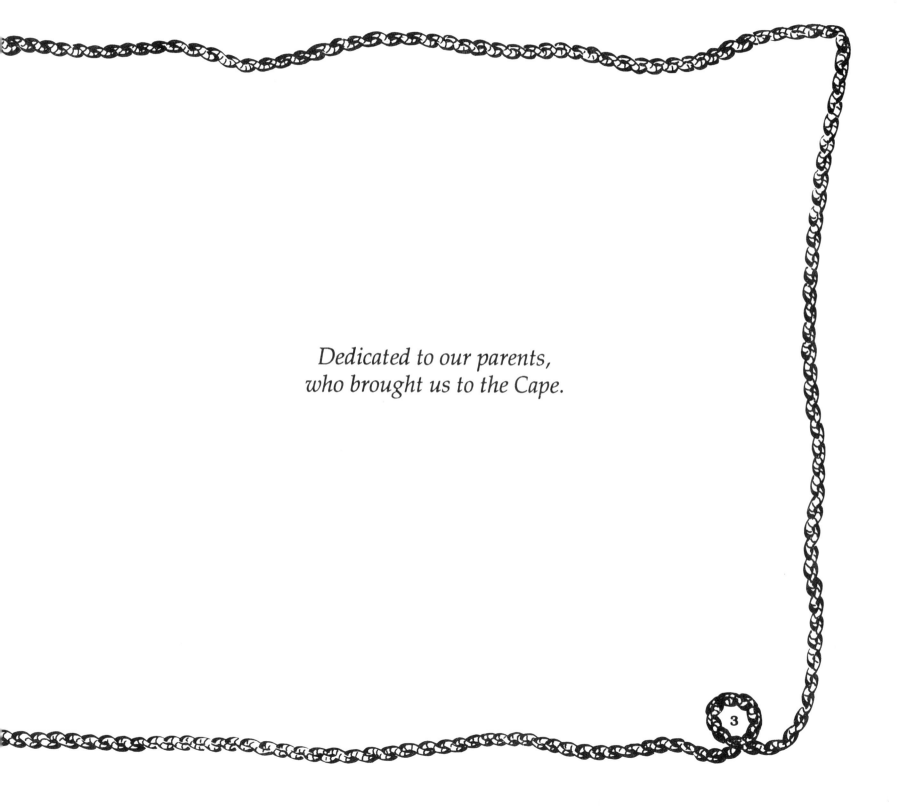

Dedicated to our parents,
who brought us to the Cape.

And so you are here, on the Land of Cape Cod,
Where the whalers and sailors, and hermit crabs trod.
You can see the smooth shore, with its soft sandy beach,
And the motion filled ocean, where playful whales breach.

But perhaps you don't know, the tale of this land,
For the tale of Cape Cod, is as old as the sand . . .

Our story begins, when the Earth was all new,
Continents forming, skies turning blue.
Where Cape Cod would be, was just smoke and steam,
With red flowing lava, forming great burning streams.
No creatures walked, no ocean flowed.
Just the sun and the moon, and the volcano's red glow.

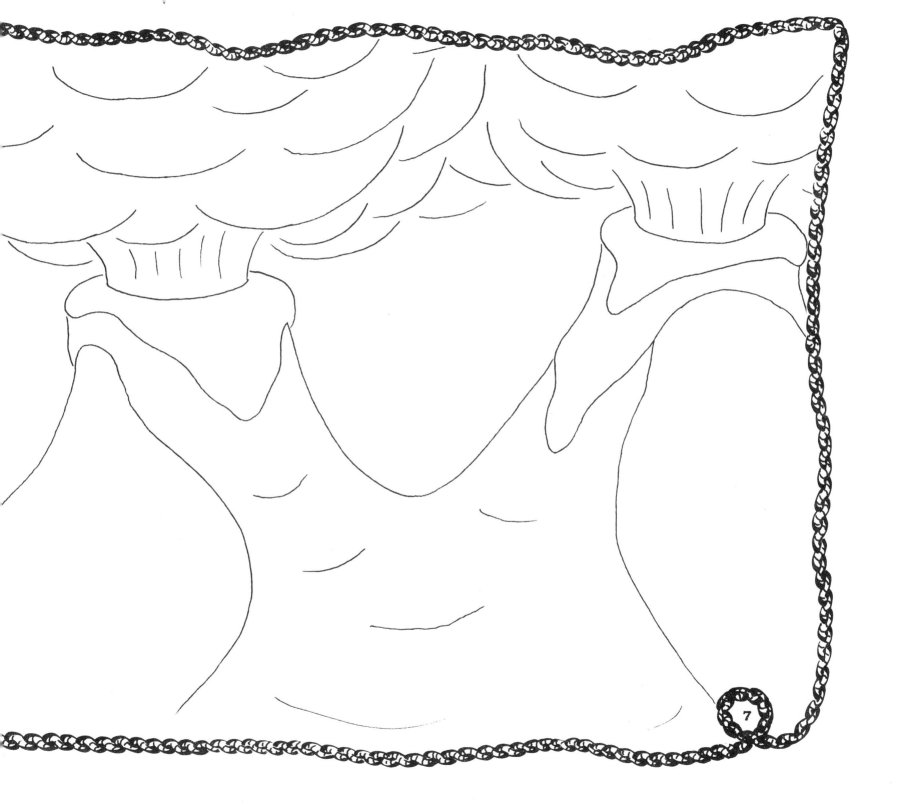

After some years, a billion or so,
Old fossils and clues, tell us what we now know.
A great ancient ocean, covered up the Cape's earth,
With huge splashing monsters, submerged in the surf.

There wasn't much land here, in dinosaur days,
Just small swampy islands, green plants and hot haze.

9

By one million B.C., the monsters were done,
With the sands of time turning, a new age was begun.
An age filled with ice, and freezing degrees,
With white snowy storms, and a deep chilling breeze.

There were mile high mountains, of ice in the sky,
And slow whooly mammoths, wandering by.

But change came again, the mammoths were gone,
The big freeze was over, warm days were to dawn.
Those mountains of ice, were melting away,
Moving more north, with each warmer day.
Those glaciers were heavy, they tore up the land,
Carving and shaping, with a cold heavy hand.

When the sculpting was done,
　　　and the cold land had thawed,
What was left was the land,
　　　that we now call Cape Cod.

Islands to the south,
    a bay to the north,
An ocean to the east,
    it would be so hence forth.
This land we would know,
    as "The Arm In The Sea,"
Was born from the glacier,
    and was as it would be.

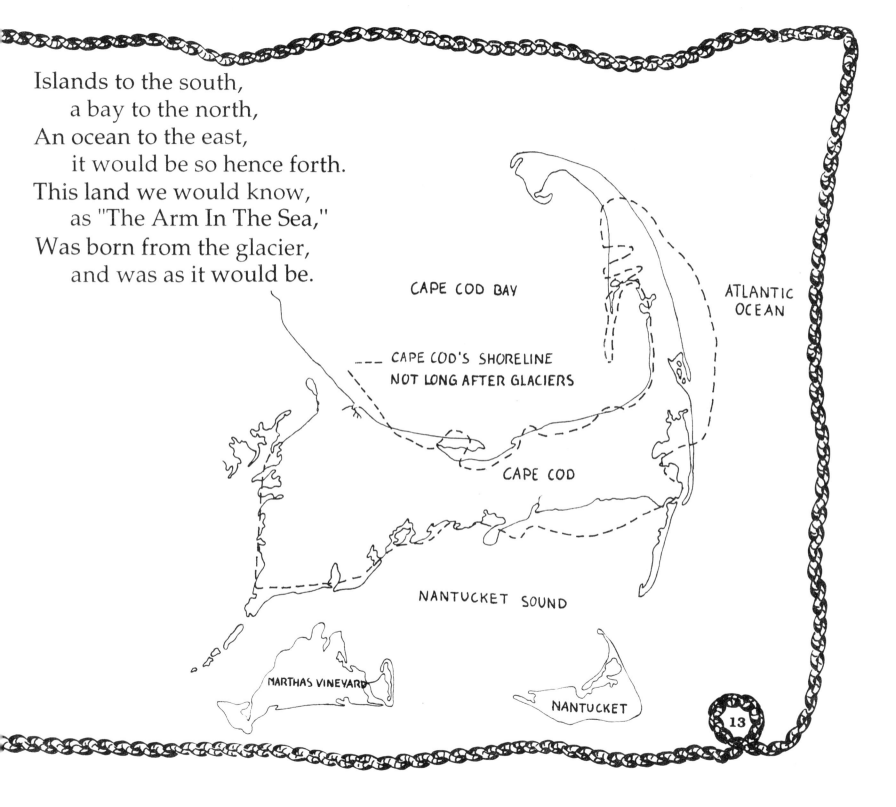

CAPE COD BAY

ATLANTIC OCEAN

--- CAPE COD'S SHORELINE
NOT LONG AFTER GLACIERS

CAPE COD

NANTUCKET SOUND

MARTHAS VINEYARD

NANTUCKET

Next came the people, hunters from the west,
Strong men searching shores, where fishing was best.
These were the first people, to step in the sand,
To discover the beauty, of a special new land.

They danced by their fires, and told stories of stars,
And legends of giants, building cliffs and sand bars.
The Wampanoag people, shared the land with the deer,
Season upon season, year upon year . . .

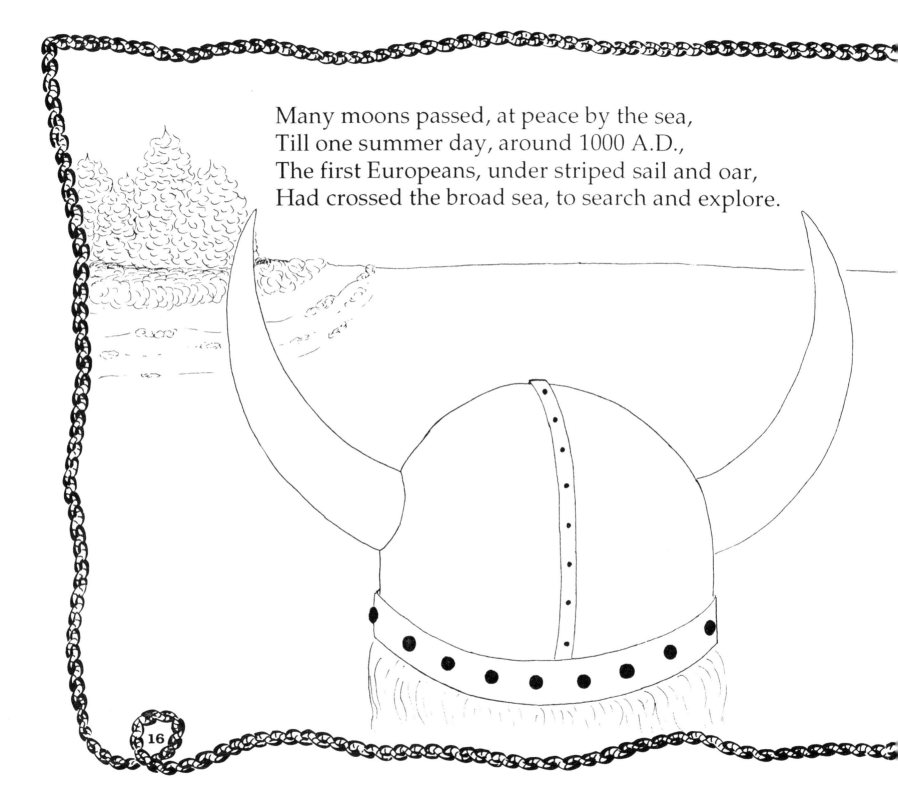

Many moons passed, at peace by the sea,
Till one summer day, around 1000 A.D.,
The first Europeans, under striped sail and oar,
Had crossed the broad sea, to search and explore.

They called the place Vinland,
    and set up a camp,
But one windy night,
    someone spotted their lamps.
Trade was attempted,
    but ended in fright,
The natives grew angry,
    there began a long fight.

That summer they stayed,
    though the Wampanoags attacked,
But the Vikings grew frightened,
    as their camp was ransacked.

And so they packed up,
    one crisp April dawn,
The redskins watched happily,
    Till the yellow hairs were gone.

They could live other places,
    lands less ill-begotten,
So the secrets and treasures,
    of this new world were forgotten.

Six hundred years after, the Vikings withdrew,
The next guest arrived, in 1602.
He'd sailed 3,000 miles, of bleak fog and cold,
This was the Englishman, Bartholomew Gosnold.

He cruised the fair shores, and sketched out a map,
He marveled at cod fish, as full nets were unwrapped.
They caught quite so many, his crew found it odd,
So dubbed he, Sir Gosnold, the fair land of "Cape Cod."

He explored the whole region, from leeward to windward,
And after his daughter, he named Martha's Vineyard.
His men stayed on Cuttyhunk, so Gosnold could roam,
But one day they told him, they missed their old home.

So he sailed back to England,
    and told of the Cape,
Where the Pilgrims of England,
    sought plans for escape . . .

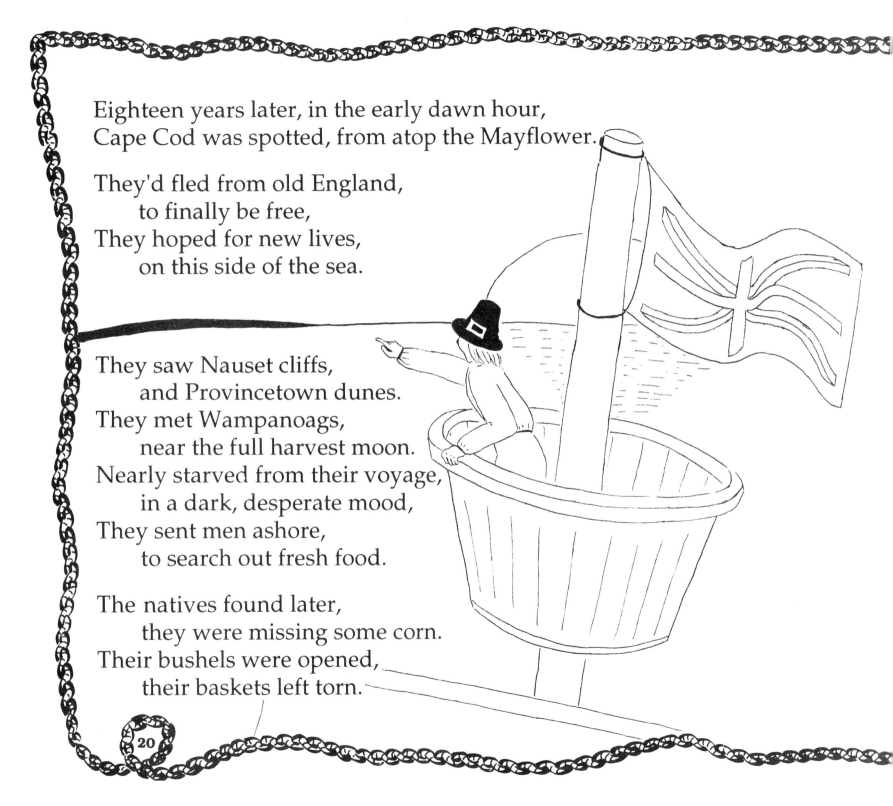

Eighteen years later, in the early dawn hour,
Cape Cod was spotted, from atop the Mayflower.

They'd fled from old England,
    to finally be free,
They hoped for new lives,
    on this side of the sea.

They saw Nauset cliffs,
    and Provincetown dunes.
They met Wampanoags,
    near the full harvest moon.
Nearly starved from their voyage,
    in a dark, desperate mood,
They sent men ashore,
    to search out fresh food.

The natives found later,
    they were missing some corn.
Their bushels were opened,
    their baskets left torn.

Angry and threatened, the natives fought back,
But no one was hurt, in the sudden attack.
So began a long conflict, on a cold Cape Cod night,
The first of many battles, between redskin and white.

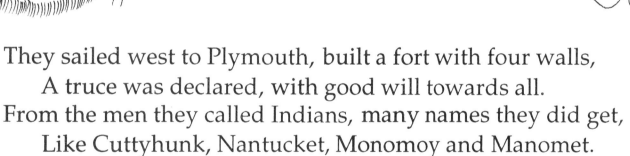

They sailed west to Plymouth, built a fort with four walls,
A truce was declared, with good will towards all.
From the men they called Indians, many names they did get,
Like Cuttyhunk, Nantucket, Monomoy and Manomet.

The first winter was hard,
    there were many who died,
But you might be related,
    to those who survived.
After one year in,
    this new way of living,
They sat down and feasted,
    the first Thanksgiving.

Many more were to follow, a great settlers' parade.
This new population, sought a place to do trade.
Someplace strategic, for swapping and sales,
Whether trading for deer skins, or oil from whales.
The Indians told them, to trade weapons or wheat,
They must come to the place, where the two rivers meet.
So in a place called Aptucxet, in present day Bourne,
The first general store, in New England was born.

In the yesteryear ways, of the Cape's early days,
Life was quite different, from what you know today.

You could sail to each harbor,
    with glass, geese and goats,
A true trader captain,
    on your own packet boat.

You could work blowing glass,
    into white and blue jars,
Or harvest sea salt,
    on the Falmouth sand bars.
You could work in a windmill,
    and harness the breeze,
Or help to pick cranberries,
    before the first Autumn freeze.

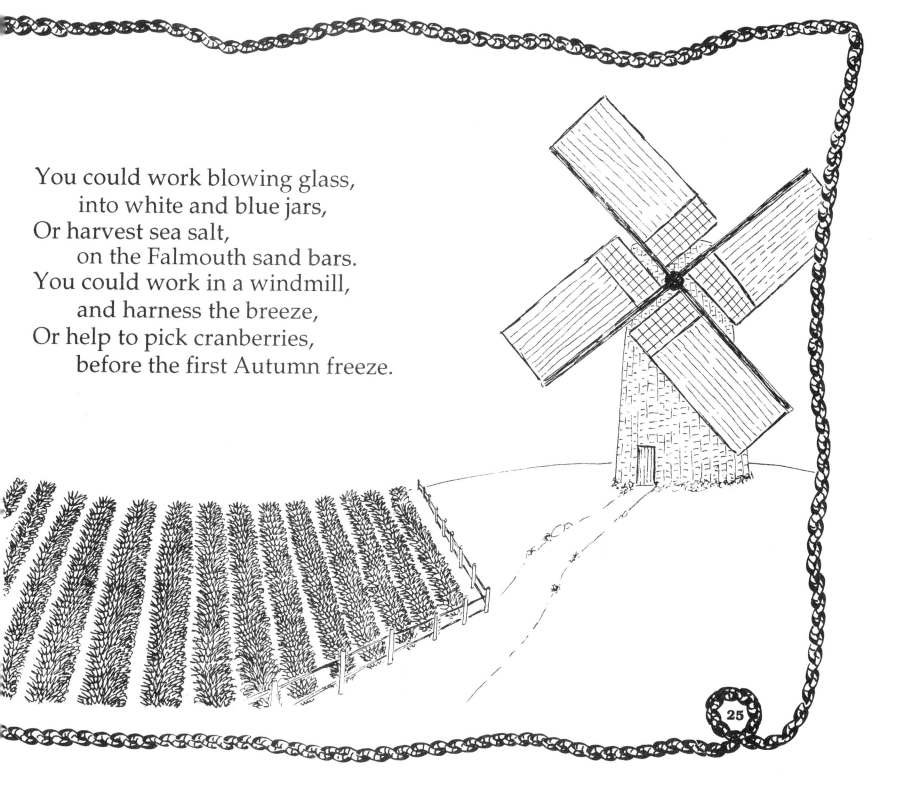

Yes, there were pirates, who spied on our shores,
Buccaneers who brought treasures, and legends and lores . . .
Some say Captain Kidd, just before he was caught,
Buried a treasure, in a dark secret spot.

Somewhere on the island, called Hog, it is said,
Lies the trunk of a pirate, long gone to the dead.
People have looked, yes people have searched,
But still south of Orleans, a lost treasure is perched.

Don't forget that old master, of the Seven Sea Felony,
That treasure rich pirate, by the name of Black Belamy.
He'd scourged the Caribbean, loaded up with his loot,
Headed north to New England, a swift escape route.
But while passing Cape Cod, and our wretched east shoals,
Black Belamy went down, with his trunks full of gold.

No one could save him, that dark stormy night,
When his ship called the "Whidah," disappeared from all sight.
She sank to the bottom, with all her dubloons,
And stayed on the bottom, for many dark moons.
But the wreck of the Whidah, did not drift away,
And gold coins wash ashore, to this very day.

In seventeen hundred, and seventy five,
The War of Independence, finally arrived.
All rebels were called, to fight tax on tea,
And the rebel cause reached, the strong arm in the sea.
At Barnstable Courthouse, brave protests and yelling,
Yarmouth made bullets, the tension was swelling.

Falmouth was fired on, by huge cannon blasts,
And Cape Codders fought back, for freedom at last.

Armed British ships, surrounded the Cape.
No food could come in, no man could escape.
But brave saboteurs, from Cape Cod would fight,
And sink British ships, in the dark of the night.

Then came a great day, for all rebel souls,
When a famed British ship, sank on our shoals.
Her Majesty's "Somerset," the pride of her fleet,
A terrible fate, on the Cape did she meet.
Stuck in the current, she swept into shore,
The hull ripped apart, with the green ocean's roar.
Top ranking officers, from the British Blockade,
Were captured and locked up, by a Cape Cod brigade.

When at last the war ended, a new nation was free,
And Cape Codders could once more, set sail for the sea.

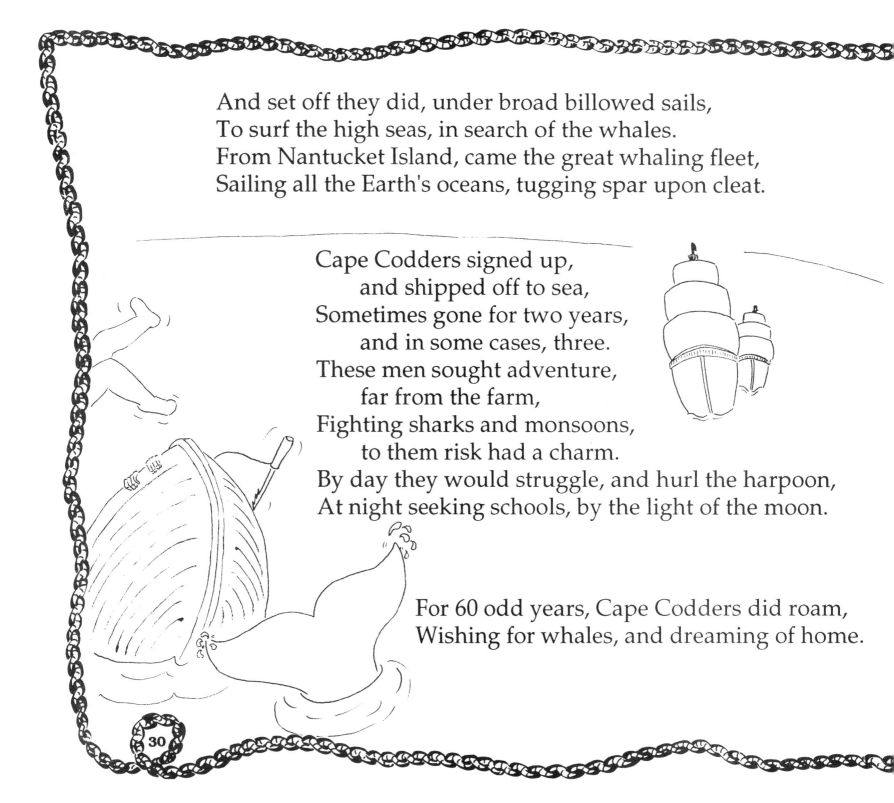

And set off they did, under broad billowed sails,
To surf the high seas, in search of the whales.
From Nantucket Island, came the great whaling fleet,
Sailing all the Earth's oceans, tugging spar upon cleat.

Cape Codders signed up,
    and shipped off to sea,
Sometimes gone for two years,
    and in some cases, three.
These men sought adventure,
    far from the farm,
Fighting sharks and monsoons,
    to them risk had a charm.
By day they would struggle, and hurl the harpoon,
At night seeking schools, by the light of the moon.

For 60 odd years, Cape Codders did roam,
Wishing for whales, and dreaming of home.

Herman Melville was a man, who signed up with the fleet,
To learn the Earth's oceans, and gain seaman's feet.
He heard legends of whales, who sank ships with a kick,
And wrote down a story . . .

the great "Moby Dick."

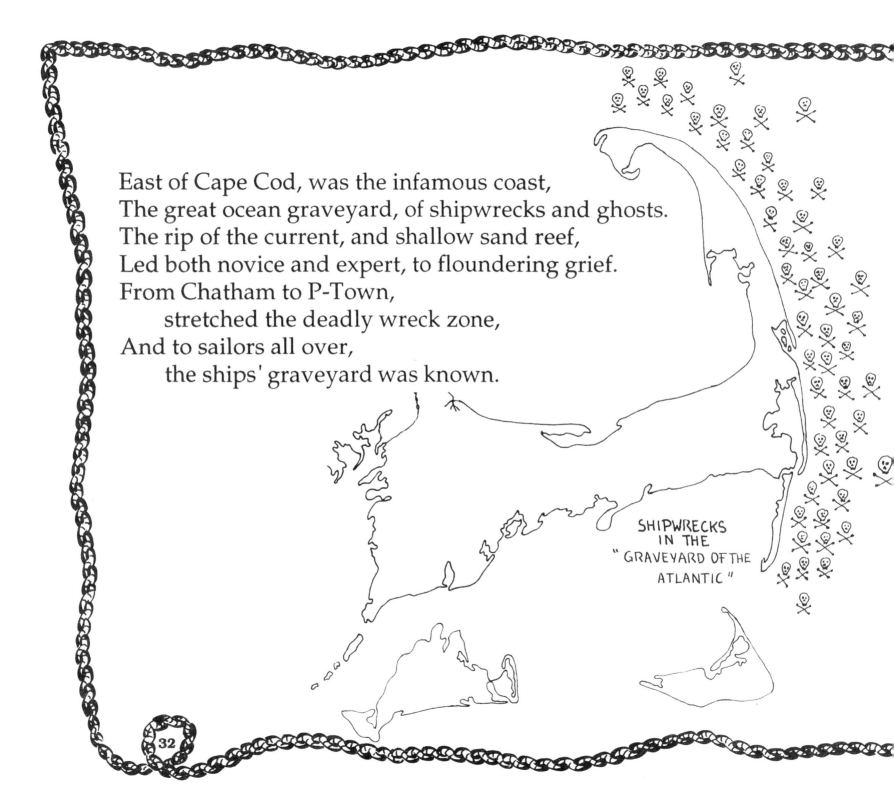

East of Cape Cod, was the infamous coast,
The great ocean graveyard, of shipwrecks and ghosts.
The rip of the current, and shallow sand reef,
Led both novice and expert, to floundering grief.
From Chatham to P-Town,
    stretched the deadly wreck zone,
And to sailors all over,
    the ships' graveyard was known.

SHIPWRECKS
IN THE
"GRAVEYARD OF THE
ATLANTIC"

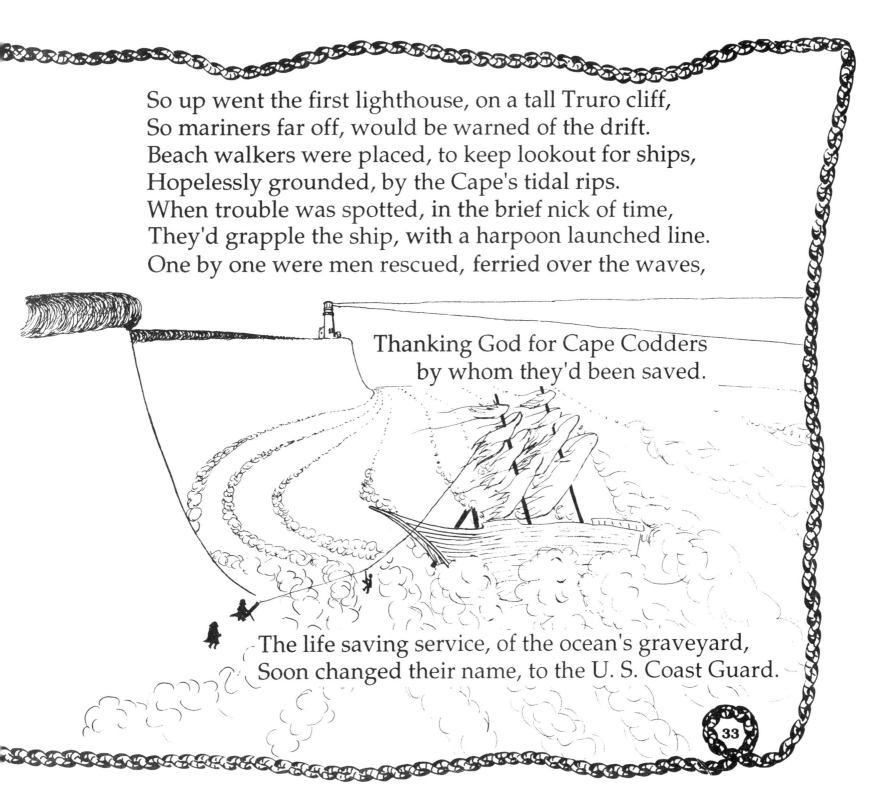

So up went the first lighthouse, on a tall Truro cliff,
So mariners far off, would be warned of the drift.
Beach walkers were placed, to keep lookout for ships,
Hopelessly grounded, by the Cape's tidal rips.
When trouble was spotted, in the brief nick of time,
They'd grapple the ship, with a harpoon launched line.
One by one were men rescued, ferried over the waves,

Thanking God for Cape Codders
by whom they'd been saved.

The life saving service, of the ocean's graveyard,
Soon changed their name, to the U. S. Coast Guard.

33

The stage coaches rolled, along the bayside,
From Sandwich to Brewster, a dust throwing ride.
The first summer tourist, bumped along with this load,
Travelers from Boston, on our first major road.
Inns were constructed, new folks could drop in,
From the posh Daniel Webster, to the Old Yarmouth Inn.
This road still exists, as the winding 6A,
Back then the rich travelers, called it "King's Highway."

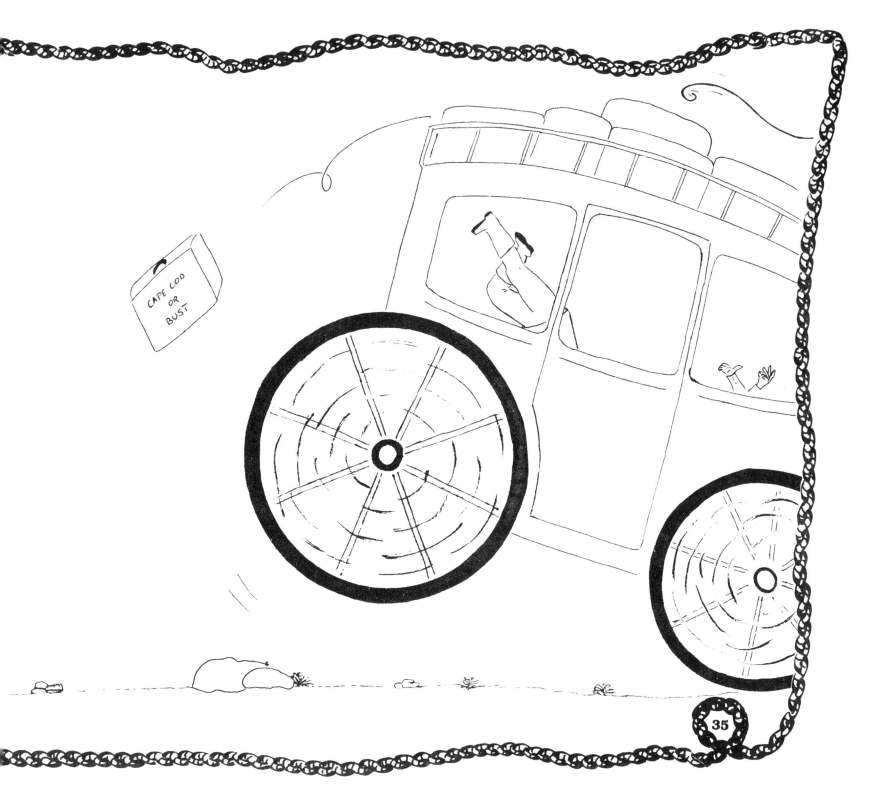

One summer traveler, who bumped along to and fro,
Was a writer from Concord, Henry David Thoreau.
He wrote of the Cape's beauty, in his thoughtful new book,
It was read by so many, that more came to look.

A later book by H. Beston, gained Cape Cod more fame,
As a quiet "time out," from the big city game.
"The Outermost House," was a tale of the beach,
About living alone, in a shack out of reach.

So began a tradition, of artists on Cape,
It was a place that inspired, to dream and escape.
A colony of artists, flooded outer Cape towns,
Painting Uncle Tim's Bridge, or a seaside sundown.

In the mid 1800s, tracks were laid down,
And the loud locomotive, hit the Cape's lucky towns.
All over Cape Cod, the steam puffed and swirled,
And Cape Cod was connected, to the rest of the world.

President Cleveland, old chief of our nation,
Had for his visits, built Gray Gables station.
Like him many more, would step in our sand,
Cape Cod was now famous, a vacationland.

Though the locals would welcome, the warm weather comers,
There was more to Cape Cod, than what happened in summers.
Strong Yankee traditions, led the worker's hard life,
The farmer, the fisherman, the innkeeper and wife.
But if one Cape profession, had a good right to gloat,
Cape Codders sure knew, how to build a good boat.
Like a cat who would always, land flat on her feet,
The catboat of Crosby's, was the pride of our fleet.
No matter what weather, nor how strong the breeze,
The catboats were calm, sailing upright with ease.
Any boat still afloat, when the rest would capsize,
Was a dollar well spent, to a true Yankee's eyes.
The grace of her sails, and the curve of her hull,
Were more common on Cape, than the Eastern Seagull.

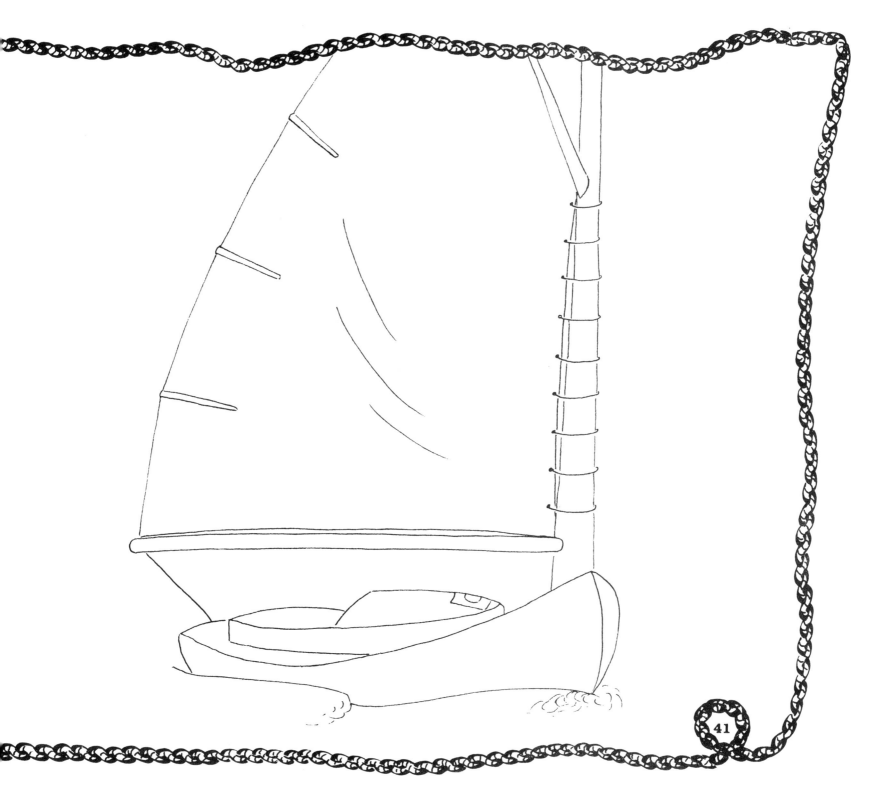

Did you know that a cable, stretched from Orleans to France,
Which was hailed as a marvelous, communications advance?
It could send and take messages, both broad and precise,
The world's first trans-Atlantic, transmission device!
So for the first time, you could send news away,
And it reached overseas, with just seconds delay.
All the big news of Europe, came through on that line,
Shooting 3,000 miles, shoreline to shoreline.

And then came Marconi, in 1903,
Whose machine could make messages, fly over the sea.
Now faster than someone, could have a note written,
The wireless message, would zoom to Great Britain.

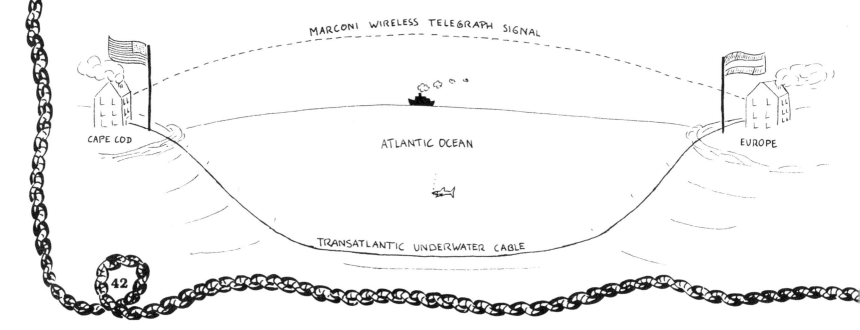

Did you know the one place in America attacked,
By World War I forces, was Orleans in fact?
A German sub surfaced, for a coastal showdown,
It shot up some boats, then aimed at the town.

Some think that this U-boat, from the bold German nation,
Was sent to destroy, the Orlean's cable station.
But they never found out, where the station was placed,
Disguised as a house, all their bombs went to waste.

And then came the gadgets, the switches, the lights,
The gas powered motors, the high biplane flights.
The crystal set radios, with dials and knobs,
The telegraph, telephone, and other thingamabobs.

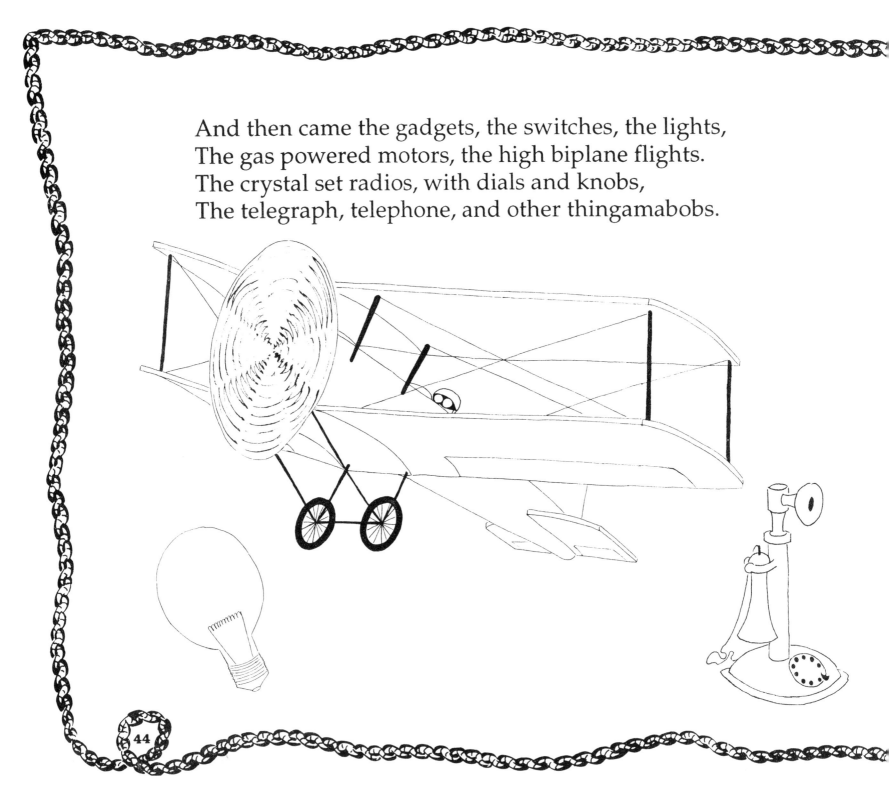

So too came the auto, which you cranked on by hand.
Then of course the first car, got stuck in Cape sand.
Paved roads were needed, so paved roads were put down,
From Woods Hole to Wellfleet, and on to P-Town.

Here's something amazing, which I'm sure you'd not think,
But imagine an island, which could suddenly sink!
An island with a lighthouse, some homes and a school,
Went down in our bay, like a rock in a pool.
It's true, I'm afraid, that old Billingsgate,
Submerged like Atlantis, to its undersea fate.
It served as a pasture, and a village to live,
But 100 years, was all she could give.
No lives were lost, so suffer no fears,
The drastic erosion, took sixty odd years.

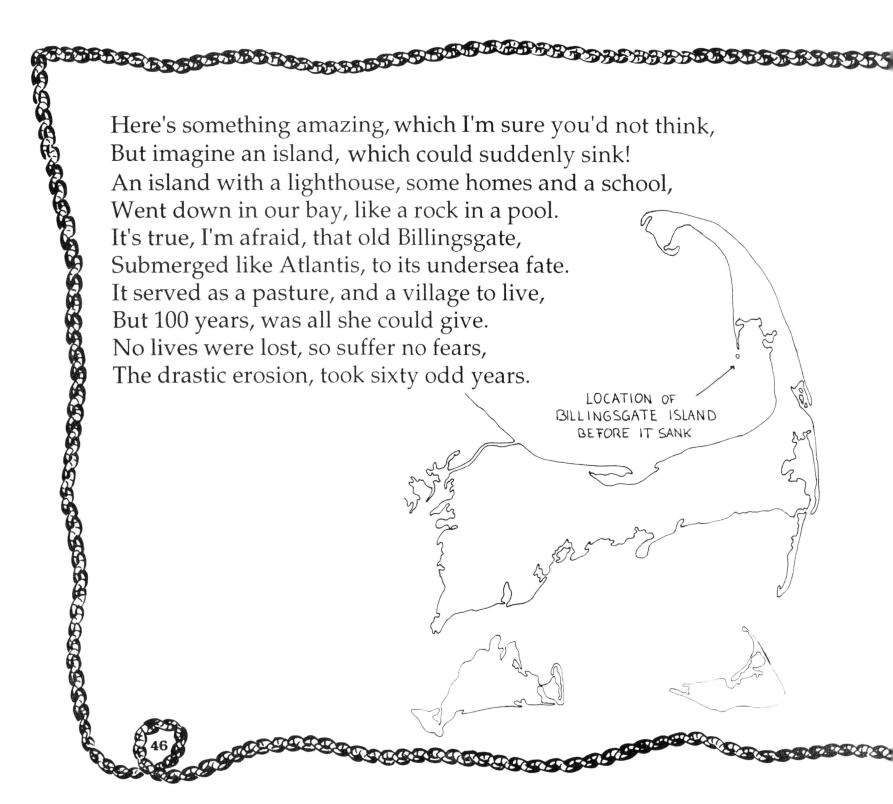

LOCATION OF
BILLINGSGATE ISLAND
BEFORE IT SANK

Around the same time, as the island went down,
A project was started, to dig up some ground.
To take an old sea route, and shorten its shape,
To dig a long channel, straight 'cross the Cape.
It had been quite a while, since the first man complained,
Of the long, risky trip, 'round the Cape's coastal lanes.

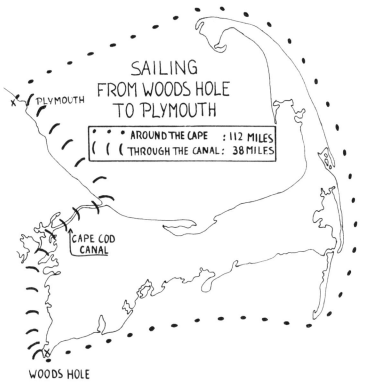

SAILING
FROM WOODS HOLE
TO PLYMOUTH

| AROUND THE CAPE | : 112 MILES |
| THROUGH THE CANAL: | 38 MILES |

PLYMOUTH

CAPE COD
CANAL

WOODS HOLE

To sail 'round Cape Cod, added days to their trip,
And the east coast had always, that deadly strong rip.

So they dug out a short cut, to shorten the ride,
Forty feet deep, and 500 feet wide.
Then up came the bridges, with their highway wide lanes,
Two for the autos, and one for the trains.

Now the Cape was an island, separated by sea,
Surrounded by waters, as an island should be.

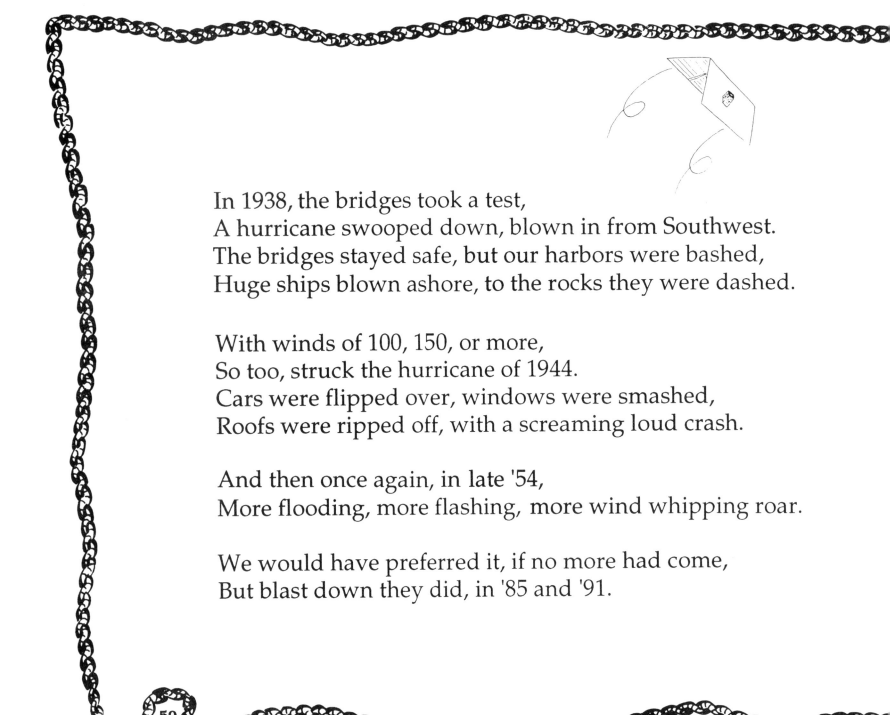

In 1938, the bridges took a test,
A hurricane swooped down, blown in from Southwest.
The bridges stayed safe, but our harbors were bashed,
Huge ships blown ashore, to the rocks they were dashed.

With winds of 100, 150, or more,
So too, struck the hurricane of 1944.
Cars were flipped over, windows were smashed,
Roofs were ripped off, with a screaming loud crash.

And then once again, in late '54,
More flooding, more flashing, more wind whipping roar.

We would have preferred it, if no more had come,
But blast down they did, in '85 and '91.

So beware of dark clouds, in the late summer sky,
Swirling 'round in confusion, with a calm sunny eye.

One house that never, was blown from the ground,
Is the house of one family, the Kennedy Compound.
Our 35th president, sailed here as a hobby,
With the Attorney General, his kid brother Bobby.
It seemed no solution, was too hard to reach,
For the president who solved problems, while walking the beach.

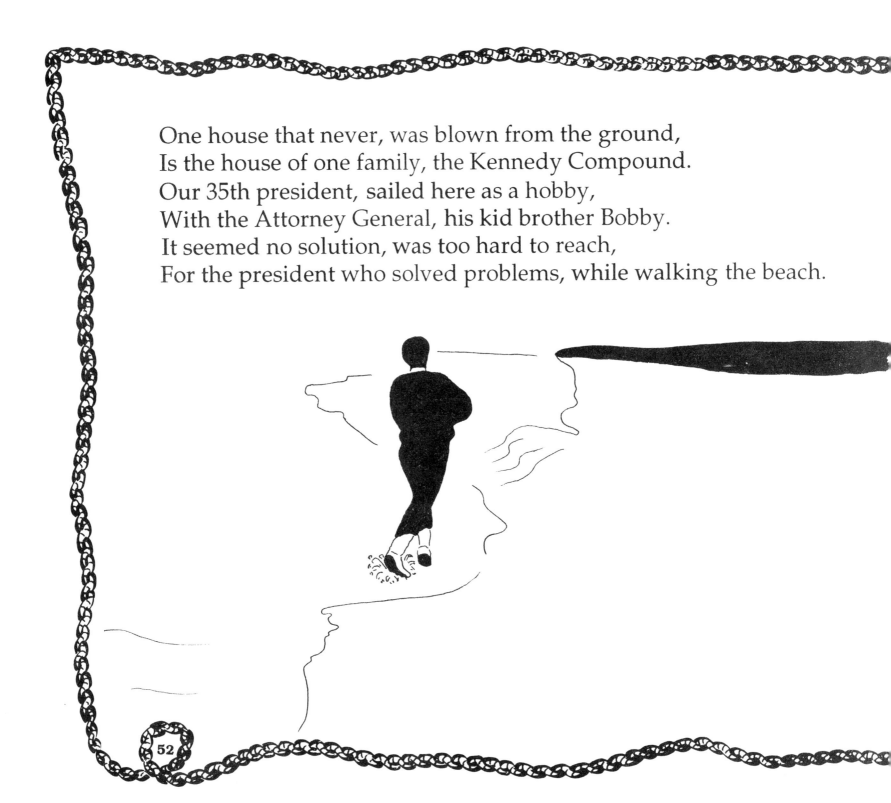

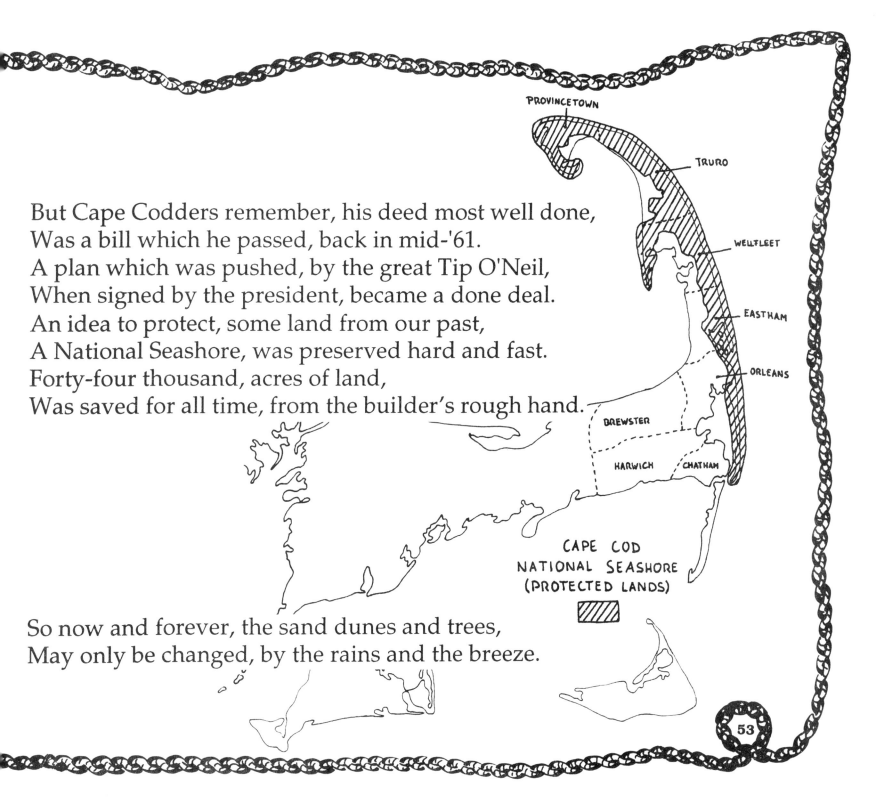

But Cape Codders remember, his deed most well done,
Was a bill which he passed, back in mid-'61.
A plan which was pushed, by the great Tip O'Neil,
When signed by the president, became a done deal.
An idea to protect, some land from our past,
A National Seashore, was preserved hard and fast.
Forty-four thousand, acres of land,
Was saved for all time, from the builder's rough hand.

So now and forever, the sand dunes and trees,
May only be changed, by the rains and the breeze.

PROVINCETOWN

TRURO

WELLFLEET

EASTHAM

ORLEANS

BREWSTER

HARWICH   CHATHAM

CAPE COD
NATIONAL SEASHORE
(PROTECTED LANDS)

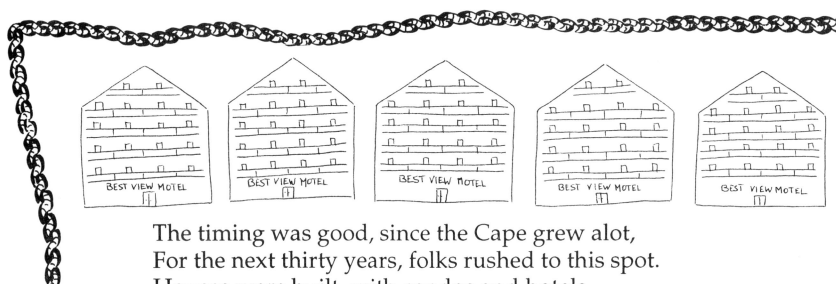

The timing was good, since the Cape grew alot,
For the next thirty years, folks rushed to this spot.
Houses were built, with condos and hotels,
And sign after sign, for the "best view motels."
Everyone squeezing, to shove more in less space,
Till all gift shops and mini golfs, had their own special place.
More trucks, more buses, mini malls with their mobs,
More traffic, more blacktop, more trash throwing slobs.
On Route 28, from Bourne to Orleans,
The developers developed, vacationland scenes.

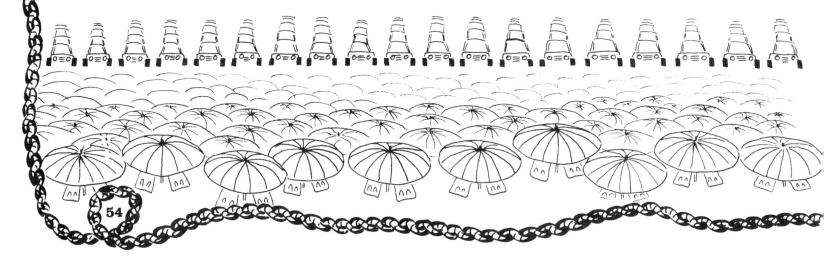

But Cape Codders fought back, and the building slowed down,
With new regulations, voted in by the towns.
Newcomers are welcome, welcome Jane, welcome Joe,
But save some green places, for our children to grow.

Like the boat builders, of a century before,
Creative Cape Codders, worked hard at their chores.
Submarine scientists, who worked in Woods Hole,
Had built a small wonder, with a deep diving goal.
A new fangled sub, with some undersea eyes,
And a robot for diving, of the small yellow size.
They named the thing "Alvin," then sank him below,
More than two miles down, where no man could go . . .

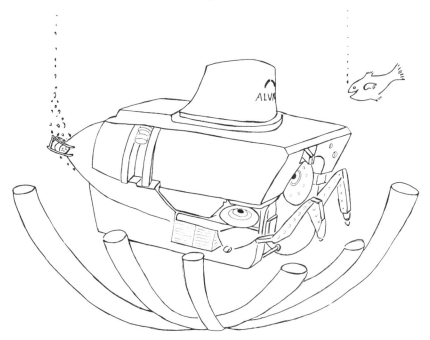

Diving deeper and deeper, to depths of unknown,
They found giant tube worms, the first time ever shown.

But they didn't stop there, those deep searching eyes,
One day came across, a sunken surprise . . .
In July '86, in the chill North Atlantic,
Alvin dove down, to explore the Titanic.

Today on Cape Cod, there's great fun to be had,
Go surfing with Mom, go fishing with Dad.
The Museum of Natural History, in Brewster is nice,
With snails and rare shells, red lobsters and mice.
You could sail out of P-Town, on a whale watching trip,
Or explore the east shore, for an old sunken ship.

There's Plimoth Plantation, and Heritage Plantation,
The Aptucxet Trade Post, old store of our nation.
Ride the smooth rails, of a cool Cape Cod train,
Or look down from above, in a sightseeing plane.

And if all of these things, seem too hard to reach,
Then do like the Vikings . . .

hang out at the beach.

Now in race the waves, under foamy white curls,
Sending splashy fun surf, for the boys and the girls.
As you play on the beach, dig your toes in the sand,
And think of the others, whose toes touched this land.
Think of the Pilgrims, the Wampanoags, the Vikings,
Think of warm summer days, and nor'easter lightnings.
Consider the past, and all it has taught,
But so too must the future, be with you in thought.
Think of the sand, as it weathers away,
And shifts to new places, with each waking day.
And hope the new buildings, which cover the land,
Will respect and preserve, our history-rich sand.

The Story of Cape Cod

1	70 Million BC	Cretaceous rock from the time of the dinosaurs.
2	10,000 years ago	Highest ground left by glacier.
3	5,500 B.C.	Earliest evidence of Native Americans on Cape Cod. Archaic period; hunter, gatherers.
	1000 B.C. - 1500 A.D.	Woodland period; bow & arrow, farming, pottery.
4	Present Day	Wampanoag Settlement.
5	1004 AD	Legendary Viking camp.
6	1602	Barthomew Gosnold's camp.
7	1620	Pilgrims first landing site.
8	1627	Aptucxet Trading Post.
9	1699	Captain Kidd's treasure chest.
10	1717	Black Belamy's sunken treasure ship, "The Whidah."
11	1760 - 1830	Golden age of whaling on Nantucket.
12	1776 - 1870	Falmouth Saltworks.
13	1778	Wreck of Her Majesty's "Somerset."
14	1779 & 1814	Falmouth Harbor attacked by British.
15	Late 1700s to present	Crosby's boat building yard.
16	1798	First lighthouse on Cape Cod, the Highland Light in Truro.
17	1800s	"King's Highway."
18	1825 - 1888	Sandwich Glass works.
19	1848	First train service reaches Cape Cod, (not on map).
20	1855	"Cape Cod" by Henry David Thoreau is published, (not on map).
21	1879	Orleans cable station opened up.
22	1880s	President Grover Cleveland's house at Grey Gables.
23	1901	First automobile reaches Provincetown, (not on map).
24	1903	Marconi wireless telegraph station opened.
25	1910	Pilgrim Monument erected in Provincetown.
26	1914	Cape Cod Canal opened.
27	1918	German submarine bombs Orleans.
28	1921	Cape Cod Chamber of Commerce established.
29	1928	"The Outermost House" by Henry Beston is published.
30	1929	Otis Military reservation established.
31	1929 to present	Home of President Kennedy and family.
32	1930	Woods Hole Oceanographic Intitution established.
33	1860s to 1930	Billingsgate Island washes away.
34	1934	Nickerson State Park established in Brewster.
35	1935	Sagamore Bridge, Bourne Bridge, and train bridge constructed over canal, (not on map).
36	1950	The Steamship Authority begins service between Woods Hole and Martha's Vineyard.
37	1954	Cape Cod Museum of Natural History opened.
38	1956	Plimoth Plantation opened.
39	1961	National Seashore established. Salt Pond Visitor Center.
40	1961	Cape Cod Community College established.
41	1969	Heritage Plantation opened.
42	1970	Cape Cod Mall constructed.
43	1985	"Titanic" discovered by Dr. Ballard of the Woods Hole Oceanographic Institution, (not on map).
44	1990	Cape Cod Commission established for future planning and guidance.

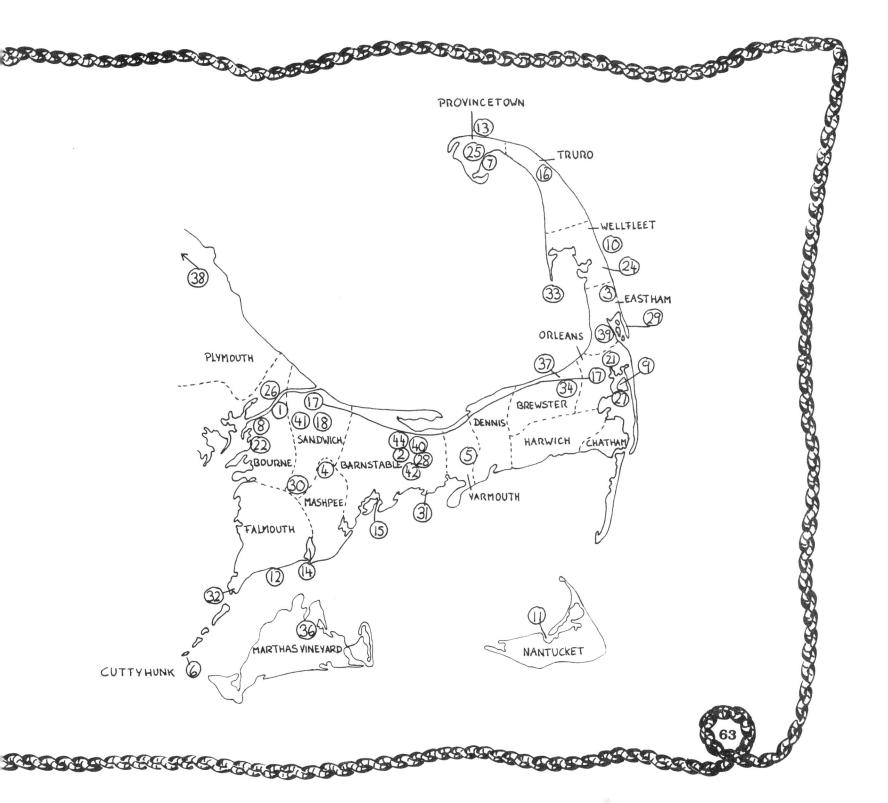

PROVINCETOWN

TRURO

WELLFLEET

EASTHAM

ORLEANS

PLYMOUTH

BREWSTER

DENNIS

HARWICH

CHATHAM

SANDWICH

BARNSTABLE

BOURNE

YARMOUTH

MASHPEE

FALMOUTH

CUTTYHUNK

MARTHAS VINEYARD

NANTUCKET

63